PARENTING DONE RIGHT IS *HARD* WORK
(But It's Worth It!)

A 31-Day Guide with Practical and Effective Parenting Tips to Win the Battle for Your Children

Tony & Nicole Davis

COPYRIGHT © 2017, 2022 – Tony & Nicole Davis

PARENTING DONE RIGHT IS *HARD* WORK (But It's Worth It!)

All Rights Reserved

GOD'S WORD is a copyrighted work of God's Word to the Nations. Quotations are used by permission. Copyright 1995 by God's Word to the Nations. All rights reserved.

Scripture quotations taken from the New American Standard Bible® (NASB), Copyright © 1960, 1962, 1963, 1968, 1971, 1972, 1973, 1975, 1977, 1995 by The Lockman Foundation. Used by permission. www.Lockman.org

All Scripture quotations, unless otherwise indicated, are taken from the New King James Version®. Copyright © 1982 by Thomas Nelson. Used by permission. All rights reserved.

Scripture quotations marked (AMP) are taken from the Amplified Bible. Copyright ©1954, 1958, 1962, 1964, 1965, 1987 by The Lockman Foundation. Used by permission.

Scripture quotations marked (NLT) are taken from the Holy Bible, New Living Translation. Copyright © 1996, 2004, 2007, 2013, 2015 by Tyndale House Foundation. Used by permission of Tyndale House Publishers, Inc., Carol Stream, Illinois 60188. All rights reserved.

Scripture quotations marked (MSG) are taken from *THE MESSAGE*. Copyright © 1993, 1994, 1995, 1996, 2000, 2001, 2002 by Eugene H. Peterson. Used by permission of NavPress. All rights reserved. Represented by Tyndale House Publishers, Inc.

Scripture quotations marked (NIV) are taken from the Holy Bible, New International Version®, NIV®. Copyright © 1973, 1978, 1984, 2011 by Biblica, Inc.TM Used by permission of Zondervan. All rights reserved worldwide. www.zondervan.com The "NIV" and "New International Version" are trademarks registered in the United States Patent and Trademark Office by Biblica, Inc.TM

Scripture quotations marked (ESV) are taken from the ESV.

This book may not be reproduced, transmitted or stored in whole or in part by any means, including graphic, electronic or mechanical without the express written consent of the publisher except in case of brief quotations embodied in critical articles and reviews. For permission requests, write to the publisher addressed, "Attention: Permission Coordinator" at the email address below.

info@empowertoengage.com ISBN 13: 9798835899760

Library of Congress Control Number: 2017964548

CONTENTS

INTRODUCTION 1
DAY 1: INTERACT WITH YOUR CHILDREN DAILY 5
DAY 2: PARENTING IS A TEAM EFFORT......................................9
DAY 3: CHILDREN ARE TO HONOR THEIR PARENTS 13
DAY 4: CHILDREN LEARN FROM OUR EXPERIENCES WITH GOD 17
DAY 5: INSTRUCT YOUR CHILDREN ACCORDING TO KNOWLEDGE 21
DAY 6: TEACH YOUR CHILDREN ABOUT GOD......................25
DAY 7: PRAY FOR WISDOM AND UNDERSTANDING TO PROPERLY INSTRUCT YOUR CHILDREN 29
DAY 8: CHILDREN SHOULD BE TAUGHT TO BE RESPECTFUL TOWARDS OTHERS 33
DAY 9: CHILDREN SHOULD BE LOVED THE WAY GOD LOVES YOU..37
DAY 10: TEACH CHILDREN THEIR IDENTITY IN CHRIST 41
DAY 11: HELP YOUR CHILDREN UNDERSTAND GOD'S INVOLVEMENT IN THEIR LIVES 45
DAY 12: EXEMPLIFY GODLY WISDOM IN DECISION MAKING BEFORE YOUR CHILDREN 49
DAY 13: RAISE CHILDREN IN AN ENVIRONMENT WHERE THE LORD IS RECOGNIZED IN DAILY EVENTS, ACTIVITIES, & CIRCUMSTANCES 53
DAY 14: PRAY FOR GOD'S DIRECTION TO PROPERLY GUIDE YOUR CHILDREN 57
DAY 15: CHILDREN CAN BE TAUGHT TO HEAR FROM GOD 61
DAY 16: ESTABLISH BOUNDARIES FOR YOUR CHILDREN...........65
DAY 17: CHILDREN ARE A GIFT FROM GOD...........................69
DAY 18: BRAND OUTWEIGHS MONEY 73

DAY 19: OBSERVE NATURAL SKILLS, TALENTS, AND ABILITIES; AND NURTURE THOSE ATTRIBUTES IN YOUR CHILDREN 77

DAY 20: BE A GODLY EXAMPLE OF RIGHTEOUS LIVING FOR YOUR CHILDREN TO FOLLOW 81

DAY 21: ESTABLISH PRINCIPLES OF GODLY LIVING SO YOUR CHILDREN WILL CONTINUE THEM ONCE THEY LEAVE HOME ... 85

DAY 22: TEACH YOUR CHILDREN TO SHOW APPRECIATION FOR OTHERS 89

DAY 23: TEACH THE WORD OF GOD TO YOUR CHILDREN 93

DAY 24: PRAY DAILY FOR STRENGTH TO BE A GOOD PARENT TO YOUR CHILDREN 97

DAY 25: TEACH YOUR CHILDREN TO SERVE OTHERS AND BE PRODUCTIVE WITH THEIR TIME 101

DAY 26: SET EXPECTATIONS FOR GROWTH 105

DAY 27: TAKE GREAT CARE IN THE WAY YOU SPEAK TO YOUR CHILDREN 109

DAY 28: LOVE YOUR CHILDREN ENOUGH TO LET THEM GO 113

DAY 29: SPEND TIME IN FASTING AND PRAYER WHEN YOUR CHILDREN FACE DIFFICULT CIRCUMSTANCES 117

DAY 30: CHILDREN SHOULD BE TAUGHT TO SERVE GOD 121

DAY 31: DO NOT NEGLECT TO HAVE THE HARD CONVERSATIONS WITH YOUR CHILDREN 125

INTRODUCTION

Unequivocally, hands down, parenting is the hardest responsibility we will EVER have! Very few explain what is required to raise a child to be an emotionally sound, kind, giving, and productive member of society.

Have you ever heard any of these sayings? "They have a mind of their own; I don't know what to do with them." "They are simply going to do their own thing." "They just do not listen to me." "I have no idea how to connect with them." With all of these challenges, most of us do not know where to go for practical help. It's almost as if we think that, by osmosis, we will just one day know what to do; and, our children will naturally fall in line and respond to whatever we say immediately and with ease—NOT!

There is a battle raging in our society for the hearts and minds of our children. They are bombarded with images of material wealth, immediate gratification, sexually enticing messaging, disrespect for authority, and an aversion to moral absolutes.

The Bible is our greatest resource for raising our children against these and other such attacks. It offers the best techniques, the best admonishments for us as parents, and the best reality-check to show us what will happen if we *don't* utilize these timeless truths. As Christians, we are without excuse for raising children who are not respectful, do not know the Scriptures, and have no sense of direction and understanding of how big and how great God is, and the difference He will make in the life of the one who whole-heartedly follows and obeys Him.

As parents, we also jeopardize the validity and power of God's Word if we are not the first partakers of it, and do not exemplify a godly way of living before our children. We will give an account for EVERYTHING we have done and have not done to properly prepare our children to exist—and live a life based on divine design.

This 31-day guide can serve as a starting place to help you understand the critical significance of your role and to show you how you need to prepare yourself to navigate parenting every day. In parenting, there are no holidays, no sick days, and no extended vacations. We are required to show up, in some form, faithfully, consistently, and be armed with the Word of God.

This easy-to-read book is designed to increase your prayer life and dependence on God in every parenting situation you face. For each day, you are provided a guiding scripture (New King James Version unless otherwise noted), a practical life-application summary with additional scriptural references, and a prayer for you to read out loud.

The initial prayer read is a supplication before God. Throughout the day, you may want to pray it again (several times) as a prayer of thanksgiving. The first time would sound like this, "God, please give me the courage to make the hard decisions to properly guide my child." This same prayer offered throughout the rest of the day would sound like this, "God, thank you for giving me the courage to make the hard decisions to properly guide my child." Feel free to add to the prayer as needed. This only serves as a starting point.

For prayers to be effective, you must first believe! There is an old adage, if you're going to pray, don't worry; but, if you're going to worry, don't pray! Prayer works only if you work it!

Some of the themes are repetitive by design. In the Bible, God talks a great deal about how to properly instruct our children and about our personal conduct as followers of Jesus Christ. And, following His example, this devotional is set up the same way. Blank pages are provided for notetaking after each day to help you capture any thoughts, ideas, questions, or additional prayer points you want to cover in your quiet time with God.

Before you begin your daily parenting devotion, purpose to give yourself ample time to read and re-read so that you can hear what the Holy Spirit is saying to you specifically about each topic. We encourage you to willfully embark upon this journey and allow the healing power of God's Word to strengthen you as a parent and create stronger relationships between you and your children. We pray you are challenged and encouraged by this 31-Day Parenting Guide.

1
INTERACT WITH YOUR CHILDREN DAILY

*Whoever brings blessing will be enriched,
and one who waters will himself be watered.*

Proverbs 11:25 (ESV)

As parents, you have to be intentional about spending quality time with your children. Whether it's working on school projects together, sharing a meal, playing a game together, or just talking about what's going on in their lives, it is important that you show your love by giving your time. Teenagers may act like they don't want your company, but they really do. Where there is resistance, explain your desire to be a part of their world because you love them and value who they are.

Interaction with your children should certainly be met with balance. We have to correct and drive out foolishness, but with tact and wisdom. You can certainly help the process by making sure that your interactions are balanced with fun and praise. You'll be bringing blessings to your children; and, as a result, you'll likewise be watered. That will provide you the strength to do it again and again.

Prayer: God, I need creative ways to spend time with my child/children. Please, put a desire in my children to want to spend time with me and to value our time above friends and social media whenever I express a desire to be together. I pray for stronger bonds with my children and only you can show me how to do it. I completely understand that quality time may outweigh quantity, so I want our time together to be meaningful. Therefore, help me to discern the appropriate course of each interaction and show me how to bring blessings that will enrich them. Thank you.

Notes

Where's Wally fun run
Activity both like have interest in
Zoo
Cafe, sit & chat
Park
Share a word, Arts & Crafts bible story, Fellas
Library
Music keyboard, guitar
Watch a mae together ask them about different
characters & what's my favour..

Notes

2

PARENTING IS A TEAM EFFORT

Having so fond an affection for you, we were well-pleased to impart to you not only the gospel of God but also our own lives, because you had become very dear to us.

1 Thessalonians 2:8 (NASB)

As parents, your familiar circle of influence will play an integral part in the development of your children. In additionto these, there will be other family members, coaches, counselors, teachers, neighbors, and others who can add parenting techniques, wisdom, and experiences beyond what you possess, and all these can help you to train and raise your child. No matter who you allow access to your children, maintain your involvement and open communication for thesafety of all involved. Create opportunities for your children to learn from people with different expertise, skills, and abilities who can expose them to different environments and greater experiences.

Prayer: God, I know that I do not know it all. And, I do not have all of the resources within myself to provide my child/children everything they need. I recognize that you did not create any of us to be self-sustaining islands. Rather, you have created us to be interdependent. So, please help me recognize the people you have selected to assist me in developing my children to be their best in every area possible. Thank you.

Notes

Notes

3

CHILDREN ARE TO HONOR THEIR PARENTS

Honor your father and your mother, so that you may live long in the land the LORD your God is giving you.

Exodus 20:12 (NIV)

As parents, honor (or respect) is demonstrated before it is taught. Teach your children what it means to honor someone by demonstrating honor towards your own parents. This is especially important if your own parents are still alive. If not, another older adult in your circle of influence will suffice.

Use your demonstration of honor as a model so that your children can have a clear understanding of God's will regarding the reverence children are supposed to have for their parents and the elderly. Additionally, when you discussrespect with your children as it relates to you, it will not be a foreign concept because you actually do it. And, it removes the inevitable judgment of hypocrisy. Similarly, there's an adage that can be applied to many situations. That adage is, "charity begins at home."

In the case of honor and respect, starting at home will provide the foundation that will be beneficial outside of the home. We are instructed to honor ALL people (1 Peter 2:17). Being respectful will open doors and help them live a long AND prosperous life.

Prayer: God, I pray that my children and I are granted long lives for following your commandments. Help me to display honor for others as well as teach my children to give honor. Help me to continually understand that granting honor is fulfilling your command; and, that is not something that parents earn. Let me display it and teach it in a way that reflects the fruit of your Spirit so that you may be glorified asthe recipient receives it.

Notes

Notes

4

CHILDREN LEARN FROM OUR EXPERIENCES WITH GOD

But watch out! Be careful never to forget what you yourself have seen. Do not let these memories escape from your mind as long as you live! And be sure to pass them on to your children and grandchildren.

Deuteronomy 4:9-10 (NLT)

As parents, you can use your personal experiences as teaching tools to reveal the faithfulness of God, the blessings of God, and the corrections of God. You know what it's like to be their age. You know the mindset. When appropriate, share your challenges and failures that lead to learning as well. Stories of your life as a Christian (or pre-Christian) can strengthen your children to stand firm and keep their faith when they are challenged through various situations.

The adage *experience is the best teacher* has a lot of truth, but it's not the whole truth. Your children can have a head start and avoid certain situations by learning from your experiences.

Prayer: God, please give me the discernment to know what my children need and when they need it. Help me to understand what they have expressed, and to understand the various layers, to get beneath the surface of what they have said to me. Moreover, provide insight into the things that they have yet to express. Grant me the wisdom to select the most appropriate experiences I have encountered with you to use them as teaching tools for my children. Thank you.

Notes

Notes

5

INSTRUCT YOUR CHILDREN ACCORDING TO KNOWLEDGE

Listen, my son, to your father's instruction and do not forsake your mother's teaching. They are a garland to grace your head and a chain to adorn your neck.

Proverbs 1:8-9 (NIV)

As parents, we are called to teach our children according to knowledge. The Scripture referenced infers that you have to communicate if your children are to listen to your instruction. That knowledge should come first from the Word of God.

Because parenting is laden with challenges at each developmental stage of a child, you are encouraged to read books and materials that can supplement your efforts to instruct your children properly and with the methods that can help you yield favorable results. Parenting done right is hardwork, but it's worth it!

Knowing that your children look to you for guidance and expect you to lead them responsibly should be enough fuel to get you to seek the best advice and increase your knowledge as you teach them. And, the older they get, the more challenging this parenting job becomes. Contrary to popular opinion, it doesn't get easier. So, as parent extraordinaire, make sure you are providing your children with solid information as they receive from you.

Prayer: God, please help me to utilize parenting information effectively and responsibly. And, reveal to me the appropriate resources to increase my understanding. Thank you.

Notes

Notes

6

TEACH YOUR CHILDREN ABOUT GOD

Teach them to your children. Talk about them when you are at home and when you are on the road, when you are going to bed and when you are getting up.

Deuteronomy 11:19 (NLT)

As parents, you are to prepare your children to face life's challenges at school, on social media, and with friends by teaching them the Word of God in a way that makes sense. The methods of teaching Bible verses may change, but the need to teach them has not. Neglecting to discuss the Bible with your children, or failing to inquire about the issues that plague young people today may be detrimental to their ability to make the right decisions. If this is an area where you are not quite sure what to do, use the internet to research ways to make learning God's Word fun and practical.

Also, do not be afraid to invade their "space." Know who their friends are, where they like to hang out, and what they are doing on social media. Doing so will give you an opportunity to know exactly what they are being exposed to. And, it will give you an opportunity to discuss how the Word of God can be used as a guide (and standard) to address any situation they face.

The reality is that our children are going to acquire information from somewhere and be influenced by someone. That information will shape their belief systems and the way they process information. The Word of God, via you as a willing vessel, may as well be the source of their information.

Prayer: God, give me witty ways to share the applicability of Your Word with my child/children. Please prepare his/her/their heart(s) to be open and receptive to learning of you. Thank you.

Notes

Notes

7

PRAY FOR WISDOM AND UNDERSTANDING TO PROPERLY INSTRUCT YOUR CHILDREN

*Wisdom is the principal thing; therefore get wisdom.
And in all your getting, get understanding.*

Proverbs 4: 7

As parents, it is important to *believe* that wisdom is the foundation for good choices and prosperity. When pursued and applied, wisdom will keep you from making mistakes you will regret. The Bible says if we need wisdom, we should just ask for it (James 1:5). Wisdom is essential. The hard truth is, before you became a parent, your child belonged to God exclusively. Allow Him to help you properly instruct the children over whom He has given you temporary stewardship. Teach them the value of wisdom and how to properly apply the principles of instruction from the Bible. Doing so will set your children up for success on earth.

Prayer: God, I thank you for allowing me to care for the child/children you have blessed me with. I need *your* wisdom in this situation. Let my children see me apply wisdom, and let that example be their standard. Please, help me recognize the difference between doing things your way and my own way. Also, give them a desire to seek your wisdom. Reveal to them the importance of your wisdom and let them see the benefits therein. Provide them with friends who likewise crave your wisdom and will not try to entice them to live lives according to the modern culture and trends that are contrary to your standards. Thank you.

Notes

Notes

8

CHILDREN SHOULD BE TAUGHT TO BE RESPECTFUL TOWARDS OTHERS

*Come, you children, listen to me;
I will teach you the fear of the LORD.*

Psalm 34:11

As parents, one of your primary responsibilities, in addition to providing food and shelter to your children, is to teach them to reverence God. Children who fear the Lord make better decisions, have higher standards, and practice self-respect. Parents teach children to fear the Lord by living with integrity. They also explain to their children how to make decisions using biblical scriptures for guidance in all their ways.

It is very important to make sure that it's understood that the fear of the Lord is the standard as you demonstrate and teach respect for the people around them. Everyone should be respected, including teachers, elderly people, authority figures, people of different nationalities, the other parent if you are not together, homeless people, and people who may not serve the same God as you.

The Bible says you cannot say that you love God, who you cannot see, if you do not love people who you *can* see (1 John 4:20). It is also true that you will not be able to respect God, who you cannot see, if you are not able to respect people you can see. Always encourage your children to ask questions and be ready to give a suitable response that encourages respecting everyone.

Prayer: God, prepare my mind and my heart to be a good example for my child/children to follow. Give me the right words to teach them to desire your path for their lives, which includes showing love and respect for others. Thank you.

Notes

Notes

9

CHILDREN SHOULD BE LOVED THE WAY GOD LOVES YOU

*Just as a father has compassion on his children,
so the LORD has compassion on those who fear Him.*

Psalm 103:13 (NIV)

As parents, your compassion for your children should require that they honor and respect you and your rules. Just as the Lord has compassion on those who fear Him, parents should take their lead from the Lord. It is reasonable to expect your children to listen to you and follow your instructions. Carefully communicate what your expectations are, and the consequences for not following your established rules.

Maintain a home that is controlled and disciplined. Your ability to consistently follow through with consequences for any defiance will set the stage for your success in this area. Compassion is also a crucial element for establishing fear (respect) and building the relationship.

Be careful not to build a culture where rewards are granted without compliance, respect, and reverence for your home and your rules. The world will not love them as much as you do, and children who do not know how to follow rules are set up for failure when it's time to navigate the world on their own. So practice establishing characteristics that will help them succeed when they leave your home.

Prayer: God, please strengthen me to establish clear boundaries for my child/children. Help me to be compassionate; and, at the same time, not allow my compassion to overrule sound judgment in the way I interact with my child/children. Thankyou.

Notes

Notes

10
TEACH CHILDREN THEIR IDENTITY IN CHRIST

Walk worthy of the calling with which you were called.

Ephesians 4:1

As parents, you are partnering with God to provide knowledge, instruction, and support to the children He has blessed you with. Like Mary, Deborah, David, and Paul in the Bible, each child has a unique assignment to help advance the Kingdom of God. You must pray to see your children the way God sees them, and you must prepare them to have godly character as they discover themselves.

They also need to be knowledgeable of the Scriptures. Their identity in Christ is far greater than their identity within your family dynamics. Prepare yourself to equip your children to respond to God's predestined calling and teach them how to learn and apply God's Word in everyday life. Encourage them to walk worthy of their calling. And, teach them to reject actions that are contrary to their calling.

Prayer: God, please help me to see what you've placed inside of my child/children. I want to do my part in preparing them for their Kingdom assignments by teaching them according to your Word. Teach me to be mindful of the treasures that are inside of them. Help me to properly communicate what you have revealed to me about them. I bind any spirits that are sent to confuse or discourage them. I pray that they obtain a greater understanding of your voice and that they will not follow any voices that are not yours. Thank you.

Notes

Notes

11

HELP YOUR CHILDREN UNDERSTANG GOD'S INVOLVEMENT IN THEIR LIVES

One generation shall commend your works to another, and shall declare your mighty acts.

Psalm 145:4 (ESV)

As parents, talk to your children about God's presence in their lives and why He should be praised. They need to understand that He is real and that they should develop their own relationships with Him. Church should not be the only place you offer praise to God or acknowledge His presence.

Living two separate and distinct lives—a church life and a separate home life—creates a hypocritical lifestyle that does not honor God. Any time you recognize God's Hand moving on your or your children's behalf throughout the day, in big and small ways, you should praise God. Teach your children to do the same by helping them recognize God's interventions, favor, and blessings.

Another way to acknowledge God's presence is by having family prayer to start each day. Teach your children to consider God in all their ways, no matter where they are. Your children follow your example far more than they listen to your words. God can use your lifestyle to shape your children to be more like Him. As this happens, they, in turn, can be used by God to influence others towards godliness as well.

Prayer: God, let my light so shine before my child/children that they will speak of my good works and give glory to your name. Increase their understanding of your involvement in their lives. Thank you.

Notes

Notes

12

EXEMPLIFY GODLY WISDOM IN DECISION MAKING BEFORE YOUR CHILDREN

*The fear of the Lord is the beginning of knowledge,
But fools despise wisdom and instruction.*

Proverbs 1:7

As parents, you must follow the Bible and purpose to walk out the principles of God before your children, even when it's hard, it doesn't seem to be working, or your faith is not as strong as it should be. Following God and being a godly example is simply a choice. Notwithstanding the fact that this choice is not always easy, it is a choice God expects us to make.

You must choose to live respectable lives. Choose to not embarrass or shame your children with your own poor decision making. Choose to be teachable and work with others such as teachers and other authority figures to model before your children that you practice obedience to the Scriptures.

It's also good to discuss your process (not the details of the problem) for making hard decisions for the family or for yourself. Children are extremely perceptive and they can see and feel when something is wrong. Be honest with your children about the need to make hard

decisions, but show them that you will make those decisions by respecting the Lord and following the guidance of the Word of God. It is wise for you to teach them the importance of making decisions through prayer and getting counsel from others who can offer sound advice. If you don't, they can be contumacious and despise the wisdom and instruction of authority.

Prayer: God, I humbly ask for your help to teach me how to talk to my children about making hard decisions and seeking you and other sound advisors for instruction when needed. By my example, help me correct any foolishness in them so that they will not despise your wisdom and instruction. Thank you.

Notes

Notes

13

RAISE CHILDREN IN AN ENVIRONMENT WHERE THE LORD IS RECOGNIZED IN DAILY EVENTS, ACTIVITIES, & CIRCUMSTANCES

Love the Lord your God with all your heart, with all your soul, and with all your strength. Take to heart these words that I give you today. Repeat them to your children. Talk about them when you're at home or away, when you lie down or get up.

Deuteronomy 6:5-8 (GW)

As parents, be consistently cognizant of the fact that you are representing the Kingdom of God. That means, for instance: watching how you react to your spouse in front of your children tempering your response to someone driving in the car next to you who cuts in front of you without using a blinker, and being mindful of critical comments you may be making about friends, relatives, or co-workers around your children.

Be an example of what it means to love God with all of your soul and strength. It's not that you can't be angry or disappointed, but your anger or disappointment should never be an excuse to use curse words or questionable behavior unbecoming of a Christian. Doing so will have a tremendous impact in turning your children's minds and hearts towards Jesus.

Use times of happiness and sadness to reflect on the love and goodness of Jesus. Express His commitment to always be a provider and a protector for your family no matter what you are facing. You are responsible for seeing Christ in every situation and likewise pointing your children to see Christ as well.

Prayer: God, please help me to always be mindful of your presence in our lives and in our home. Remind me to share of your goodness and your plan for our lives with my children. Thank you.

Notes

Notes

14

PRAY FOR GOD'S DIRECTION TO PROPERLY GUIDE YOUR CHILDREN

Trust in the Lord with all your heart, and do not lean on your own understanding. In all your ways acknowledge him, and he will make straight your paths.

Proverbs 3:5-6 (ESV)

As parents, you will experience fear, anxiety, frustration, and anger. With all of these emotions, you are still expected to seek God's counsel in how to handle each unique situation you may be faced with.

Quite frankly, it takes intestinal fortitude to follow the instructions of the Lord, when that leading does not readily jive with your own understanding. Prayer is going to be your greatest weapon. No matter how immediate or serious each issue may be, there is always enough time to pray. His still small voice can ring loud when you purpose your heart to hear Him before you act.

Trust that the omniscient God will provide the right direction for you and your children. And, be willing to go in the direction He tells you, regardless of your understanding, or lack thereof. He honestly knows where He wants you and your children to be and He knows when He wants you to be there.

Prayer: God, please show me how to trust you in every situation I am faced with as I raise my child/children. Teach me to always seek your direction. And help me to stay encouraged as you direct my children and me in ways that I may not completely understand. Thank you.

Notes

Notes

15

CHILDREN CAN BE TAUGHT TO HEAR FROM GOD

I will instruct you and teach you in the way you should go; I will counsel you with my eye upon you.

Psalm 32:8 (ESV)

As parents, you can teach your children to listen for God to speak to them. Just as young Samuel was taught to distinguish God's voice from Eli's voice in 1 Samuel 3, you too can instruct your children to know the difference between God's voice and Satan's voice when making decisions.

Talk about what they hear in their conscience and whether what they are thinking is good and helpful to self or others or bad, self-seeking, and hurtful to self or others. Proverbs 20:27(AMP) instructs us that "the spirit (conscience) of man is the lamp of the Lord."

Use the examples that Jesus used when He spoke with Peter about distinguishing the difference between his ability to hear from God versus his own mind. In Matthew 16:17, we see Jesus telling Peter that his answer was not revealed by flesh and blood but by the Father. Later, in Matthew 16:23, we see Peter being rebuked because Satan was the source of what seemed to be an innocent statement. We can teach our children to recognize the source of their thoughts as well.

Sin is enticing, so teach your children the importance of being comfortable saying, "No." It can keep them out of trouble and help them to recognize situations that can hurt them. You don't want to instill fear, but you do want to instill a level of awareness that can keep them safe when faced with making decisions when you are not present.

Prayer: God, please give my child/children sensitivity to recognize your voice. Please, help me show them in your Word the kind of instructions you give versus the kind of instructions Satan gives. Thank you.

Notes

Notes

16

ESTABLISH BOUNDARIES FOR YOUR CHILDREN

Rebuke a wise man, and he will love you.
Give instruction to a wise man, and he will be still wiser.

Proverbs 9:8-9

As parents, assess how well you do or don't receive correction or instruction, whether at home, at work, at church, or from other authority figures. If your children see that you do not follow rules or established boundaries, it will be difficult for you to enforce them.

Boundaries are important because they provide safety. And, today more than ever, parents must protect their children and teach them to follow rules and adhere to boundaries.

Parents, you will only be effective in this area to the extent that you follow your own guidance and lead by example. Help your children to understand that receiving correction will ultimately set them up for success. While no one likes to be reproved, it beats the alternative of not being corrected and continuing in your mistakes. Use examples such as coaches constantly correcting professional athletes to show that receiving correction is actually welcomed by those who want to excel. Also, explain that the converse is also true. Poverty and shame will come to those who refuse instruction (Proverbs 13:18).

Prayer: God, please help me to lead by example. In any areas of my life where I struggle with adhering to established boundaries, I want to change for the sake of my children. Help my children and me to understand that receiving correction will make us better. And, give me the capacity to continue to love those who love me enough to offer a rebuke whenever I make a mistake. Thank you.

Notes

Notes

17

CHILDREN ARE A GIFT FROM GOD

Then God said, "Let Us make man in Our image, according to Our likeness; let them have dominion over the fish of the sea, over the birds of the air, and over the cattle, over all the earth and over every creeping thing that creeps on the earth."

Genesis 1:26

As parents, it is important for you to see your children as God sees them. Fundamentally, each one of us has been created with the ability to exhibit the characteristics of God. Just as the Godhead fellowships, people have been designed to fellowship with God.

Regardless of what may be happening at the time, God sees each of us as someone who was created in His image. He is longsuffering towards us, not willing that any should perish (2 Peter 2:9).

In addition, God has a specific plan for each one of us. Yes, God has created His children to impact the world in a unique way. And, He wants them to fulfill their purpose.

Prayerfully seek God for revelation about who He has created your child/children to be. As God slowly reveals their talents, abilities, and gifts to you, be patient as you walk them through the developmental years.

Your child is a precious gift—a masterpiece. And, they are also a work in progress. While they may struggle in certain areas, remember that they were created to be the head and not the tail (Deuteronomy 28:13). Remind them of this fact even when circumstances give the appearance of another reality. You will be able to communicate this if you remember to see them as God sees them.

Prayer: God, please help me daily to see who you have created my son(s)/daughter(s) to be. Remind me that they are gifts from you, who were created in your image, just as I was. Thank you.

Notes

Notes

18

BRAND OUTWEIGHS MONEY

A good name is to be chosen rather than great riches.

Proverbs 22:1

As parents, part of your responsibility is to teach children honesty, kindness, and hospitality towards others. During the early years, it's quite easy to show children how to share and to tell them to be nice. But, as they reach adolescence, there is a strong sense of entitlement that arises along with the *me* complex. That's when children believe the world revolves around them.

No matter the age, the Bible is your resource to compel children to model themselves after Jesus and after you. Continue to talk about the importance of the *golden rule: treat others the way you wanted to be treated.* Talk about the importance of seeing a person of integrity when they look at their own reflection in the mirror. As you demonstrate these attributes, allow your children to partner with you during service activities or you partner with them. Help them to stay mindful of the fact that no matter what they are doing or where they go, they want to be good representatives of themselves, the family, and ultimately God.

Prayer: God, give me strength and capacity to give more to my children and my community and to be a positive example for my children to follow. Help me to demonstrate that a good name, my integrity, will never be sacrificed by the desire to pursue riches. Let my example resonate with them so that they will live lives of integrity too. Thank you.

Notes

Notes

19

OBSERVE NATURAL SKILLS, TALENTS, AND ABILITIES; AND NURTURE THOSE ATTRIBUTES IN YOUR CHILDREN

Train up a child in the way he should go, and even when he is old he will not depart from it.

Proverbs 22:6

As parents, you have front-row seats into the lives of your children. Observe their interests and provide them opportunities to make deeper discoveries into those interests. Help them to discover their interests. You can see much better than they can, where they seem to be naturally gifted.

When you see strong abilities, encourage your child to pursue activities and hobbies that they may first resist. By doing so, you are helping to expose them to their inner strengths and awakening their God-ordained purpose of existence. Also, you are encouraging them to discover their place on the seven mountains of cultural influence which gives them the ability to impact our world. These mountains are business, government, education, arts and entertainment, media, religion, and family. Encourage your children to pursue careers in *their* fields of choice.

Not doing so can cause them to spend many years switching back and forth between many paths that do not fit their gifts, talents, and interests. This is time that can be redeemed. Please do so. If you aren't sure how to do this, get the assistance of a coach, a mentor, a counselor, or a friend.

Prayer: God, please give me eyes to see the treasures inside my child/children that need to be unlocked. Thank you.

Notes

Notes

20

BE A GODLY EXAMPLE OF RIGHTEOUS LIVING FOR YOUR CHILDREN TO FOLLOW

And anyone who welcomes a little child like this on my behalf is welcoming me. But if you cause one of these little ones who trusts in me to fall into sin, it would be better for you to have a large millstone tied around your neck and be drowned in the depths of the sea.

Matthew 18:5-6 (NLT)

As parents, you have two options. You can raise your children according to the Word of God, or you can choose to raise your children according to some other standard. As a Christian, there is no justifiable reason to haphazardly guide your children. However, should you choose to do so, Jesus is clear in His warning.

No action or behavior taken as a parent is harmless or innocent if the outcome is a negative reaction from your child towards God. The innocence of your children must be protected. Know that your actions are being observed and more than likely, your children will imitate you. Therefore, do not do anything that will cause your children to sin. It is not good for them. And, it is not good for you. The example that you demonstrate to your children is serious business.

Prayer: God, help me to always be mindful of my parenting responsibilities, and the fact that I am always being observed. Help me to represent you well and instill godly characteristics in my children that will influence them in ways that are pleasing to you. Thank you.

Notes

Notes

21

ESTABLISH PRINCIPLES OF GODLY LIVING SO YOUR CHILDREN WILL CONTINUE THEM ONCE THEY LEAVE HOME

Tell your sons about it, and let your sons tell their sons, and their sons the next generation.

Joel 1:3 (NASB)

As parents, you have a wonderful opportunity to establish traditions, standards of living, and principles of daily conduct that can follow your children into adulthood. Quite frankly, itis your responsibility. If you fail to do so, your children will not be able to carry on a godly legacy that reaches generations to come. Remember, we are to leave an inheritance to our children's children (Proverbs 13:22).

Determine the godly principles that will serve as hallmarks for the way your home functions and communicate those to your children. Establish biblical sayings that can be used during difficult times. Let such maxims be those that are short and easy to remember, such as, "I know God has a plan for you"(Jeremiah 29:11) or "With God, all things are possible" (Matthew 19:26). Practice them so that they may get in the hearts of those that hear them. Show how the Word can be applied. And, make sure to discuss the *whats* and *whys* of your decisions.

Prayer: God, please bless and multiply our family as we uphold your Word when we're apart. Help us to establish the godly traditions that can be passed from generation to generation. Thank you.

Notes

Notes

22

TEACH YOUR CHILDREN TO SHOW APPRECIATION FOR OTHERS

It is the living who give thanks to You, as I do today;
A father tells his sons about Your faithfulness.

Isaiah 38:19 (AMP)

As parents, teach gratitude to your children. It starts with common courtesy, then builds to acts of kindness for the good things people have done. Teenagers do not get a pass in this area. Parents should keep a watchful eye to ensure teenagers are being appreciative and thanking others for both small and large acts of kindness. It can start small. "Please" and "thank you" are important words. Use them often with your children and they will use them often with others.

Be mindful of the fact that gratitude goes both ways. So, parents should also demonstrate gratitude to their children. In addition to showing appreciation with our mouths, it is also important to have a thankful heart. The words spoken from an authentic heart will certainly have more of an impact.

Prayer: God, please give me a generous heart. Help me to remember to say please and thank you to my children often so they can learn these acts of gratitude. Thank you

Notes

Notes

23

TEACH THE WORD OF GOD TO YOUR CHILDREN

How can a young person stay on the path of purity?
By living according to your word.

Psalm 119:9 (NIV)

As parents, you learn the Word of God to help yourself and to teach your children. It may be hard to believe, but even *your* children will be tempted to pursue many avenues that are contrary to the standards of the Scriptures. They will see many people who succeed by pursuing those alternative, ungodly methods. Yet, it must be established that God's way is the best way—period.

The best way to establish this truth is to be a good example before them. And, the Word of God is your greatest weapon and defense to help your children stay integral and pure before Him. The Word complimented with your consistent Godly- lifestyle can encourage your children to remain true and committed to your teachings and the path that is straight and narrow (Matthew 7:13-14). The Word works if you work it with no deviations or justifications for straying from God's path. Be consistent with your words and deeds as you live according to His Word.

Prayer: God, ignite in me a passion and hunger for your Word. I want to be used as your ambassador to live and teach your Word to my child/children. Let my spirit always be receptive to your wisdom as it cries out to me. I know that doing so will keep me pure and provide my child/children an example of living according to your Word, which is the only way to keep ourselves on the path of purity. Thank you.

Notes

Notes

24

PRAY DAILY FOR STRENGTH TO BE A GOOD PARENT TO YOUR CHILDREN

I can do all things through Christ which strengthens me.

Philippians 4:13

As parents, you have the single most important job on the planet. You are responsible for the well-being of another human being. From birth, the very lives of those children are in your hands. When you think about it, it can be quite overwhelming at times. Issues such as being in unfamiliar waters as a parent, not understanding the unique challenges of the culture, and finances can simply make you feel downright inadequate.

God has given us everything we need to be successful in our roles. Your strength comes from God, not from your own attempts. If you look to God, the job of parenting does not have to be unbearable—yes, it's challenging, but not unbearable. Human strength will fail you, but God-given strength will sustain you.

Prayer: God, please give me your strength to be the best parent I can be. I'm willing to grow and change to fulfill this assignment as you require. Thank you for never leaving nor forsaking me. And, thank you for sending the Holy Spirit as my Comforter, Advocate, Intercessor, Standby, and Strengthener.

Notes

Notes

25

TEACH YOUR CHILDREN TO SERVE OTHERS AND BE PRODUCTIVE WITH THEIR TIME

Our people must also learn to engage in good deeds to meet pressing needs, so that they will not be unfruitful.

Titus 3:14 (NASB)

As parents, your schedule may not always permit substantial oversight of your children, especially if they are teenagers. As a part of developing good time management skills, it is important to help your children be productive with their time. It's easy to spend hours in front of a television, chat idly with friends, or spend a great deal of time on some type of electronic device.

While they certainly need space for entertainment and relaxation, they must also redeem their time and be mindful not to waste it. As the parent, it is necessary to monitor what your children are doing and help them establish meaningful ways to help others. Instruct them that it is rewarding to engage in good deeds towards others and that it is more blessed to give than to receive (Acts 20:35).

Prayer: God, as I challenge my child/children to spend time being more productive, please lessen the likelihood of resistance and replace it with a spirit of receptivity. Thank you.

Notes

Notes

26

SET EXPECTATIONS FOR GROWTH

Therefore let us leave the elementary doctrine of Christ and go on to maturity.

Hebrews 6:1 (ESV)

As parents, you must not hesitate to challenge your children. It is important to challenge them to continue to improve in various aspects of their lives, and that includes their knowledge of the Word of God. While everyone learns at their own pace, growth is still expected. If your children's primary involvement with Scripture is during church services, consider setting aside planned times of Bible discussion at home.

It is also good to use Scripture when addressing situations in the home to teach your children how to practically apply the Word of God to real life situations. As you observe their natural talents, encourage them to develop those talents into a worthwhile skill. Start with fundamentals and prepare them to conquer their mountain of influence as outlined on Day 19.

Prayer: God, open additional opportunities for me to discuss your Word with my child/children. Help me to not embrace lack of growth. Continue to speak to my heart to grow in you, and I will encourage and challenge my children to do the same. Thank you.

Notes

Notes

27

TAKE GREAT CARE IN THE WAY YOU SPEAK TO YOUR CHILDREN

Words kill, words give life; they're either poison or fruit—you choose.

Proverbs 18:21 (MSG)

As parents, it is imperative that you remain conscious of the fact that you have a tremendous impact on your children's lives. Most adults remember the positive words that were spoken to them and the positive impact that those words had on them as they grew up. Likewise, most adults also remember the negative ones and the negative impact of those words spoken to them.

You may notice that you often speak to your children the way your parents spoke to you. This is only acceptable if you were raised by God-fearing parents who took counsel from this scripture in Proverbs. If not, assess the kind of words you use and observe the impact of those words on your children. If your words are not edifying and uplifting, you must change this immediately. This is an area that requires a modified approach. The seeds you plant will be the fruit you harvest.

Prayer: God, keep me mindful of the fact that my words have the power to produce either fruit or poison in the lives of my children. Help me to bridle my tongue and to speak positive words that will produce fruit and not poison in the life of my children. In those times where I have been careless, please forgive me for using unedifying words towards my children. I want to do better and I will with your help. Thank you.

Notes

Notes

28

LOVE YOUR CHILDREN ENOUGH TO LET THEM GO

When I was a child, I talked like a child, I thought like a child, I reasoned like a child; when I became a man, I did away with childish things.

1 Corinthians 13:11 (AMP)

As parents, one of the hardest experiences you will face as your child develops and matures is letting go. You will endure this process many times: through grade school, high school, the military, college or trade schools, and adulthood. What will help you to not transfer your fears, inhibitions, and self-assigned boundaries to your child is remembering that ultimately your child does not belong to you.

God has called your child to fulfill a specific assignment in the earth. While you will always be their parent, childrearing is seasonal. And, that season in your home will eventually come to an end. The personality, interests, and talents given to your child were uniquely designed for God's Kingdom work.

Encourage your children to prepare for their futures and to embrace their growth by putting away childish things (in the appropriate time) as they grow. As a side note, be mindful of your own transitions as your children prepare to leave your home. By doing so, you can have peace and acceptance for the inevitable and needful transition. Let them grow and go.

Prayer: God, help me learn to celebrate and not lament the changing seasons of parenthood. I embrace the fact that my children will leave home. And, I am excited to embark on new opportunities that you have for me as I prepare to fulfill my destiny with my children out of the home. Thank you.

Notes

Notes

29

SPEND TIME IN FASTING AND PRAYER WHEN YOUR CHILDREN FACE DIFFICULT CIRCUMSTANCES

"Lord, have mercy on my son, for he is an epileptic and suffers severely; for he often falls into the fire and often into the water."

Matthew 17:15

As parents, there will be times when your children are facing a particularly hard situation or illness. In these types of situations, be ready to go above and beyond human capabilities and human resources.

First, acknowledge the reality of the situation. Don't be in denial. Jesus told us that there will be trials and sorrows on earth (John 16:33). No one is exempt from facing difficult times. Know that you can have peace in Him, and your Father can use any situation for His glory. This is true even when we do not quite understand.

Second, parents need to be prayer warriors and they need to fast. Your faith will be tested and strengthened as you look to God for answers, healing, and deliverance.

Third, it is also wise to allow others who are strong in faith to pray with you and add their faith to yours.

Prayer: God, you are my source. I need you to change this hard situation. I know you are able. I will fast and pray until you speak. Help me not to doubt, but only believe. I don't know what to do and I am desperate for your guidance. Thank you.

Notes

Notes

30

CHILDREN SHOULD BE TAUGHT TO SERVE GOD

Then God said to Abraham, "As for you, you must keep my covenant, you and your descendants after you for the generations to come."

Genesis 17:9 (NIV)

As parents, you must establish God's Word and His principles in your home.

First, you must understand your covenant with God. If you do not understand the covenant, spend time in prayer asking Him to reveal it to you. If you have knowledge of the covenant, likewise spend time in prayer, seeking direction, to make sure that you are exactly where you are supposed to be in the process. But, let's be clear about this. Understanding the covenant is not enough. We are commanded to keep His covenant.

And, there is another point that must be observed. The covenant is for you AND your descendants. If your children are going to keep the covenant, they have to first be taught about it.

Children primarily learn from you in two ways. One way is to simply make sure that you tell them. Parents should endeavor to have regular conversations with their children regarding the direction of the family.

Another way children learn is by watching. Whether you realize it or not, they are ALWAYS watching. Children do as they see, and what they see will always have a stronger impact on what you say. If you want your children to be mindful of God's omnipresence and to conduct themselves respectfully and responsibly according to His plan for their lives, use the Word of God to teach them His ways.

Prayer: God, as I look to your Word daily for guidance, please show me how I can better keep your covenant that your presence and your blessing are with my family for generations to come. Thank you.

Notes

Notes

31

DO NOT NEGLECT TO HAVE THE HARD CONVERSATIONS WITH YOUR CHILDREN

*My little children, these things I write to you,
so that you may not sin. And if anyone sins, we have an
Advocate with the Father, Jesus Christ the righteous.*

1 John 2:1

As parents, you must be ready and willing to have hard conversations with your children regarding sex, drugs, alcohol, and money. Please, note that not discussing the issues does not equate to their non-existence, and not discussing the issues does not eradicate challenges your children may be having in these areas.

Today, children are getting involved in dangerous activities in some or all of these areas. Establish open communication with your children so that you are able to sit down with them to discuss their views, their involvement, and their struggles with the lust of the flesh and the lust of their eyes. Talk directly about the issues you know they are facing. And, talk about the issues or challenges being faced by their friends.

Do not be afraid to have these hard conversations. If you need someone to help you, seek the support you need. If their friends are going through it, your child will be at least indirectly involved. You will need to involve the other parents, the school, your pastor, or anyone else needed to settle the issue and save your children! Help them to understand what it means that they have an Advocate, with the Father. He gives us the ability to live in Him just as Jesus did (1 John 2:2, 6). If you struggle in any of these areas, stop here and get help.

Prayer: God, please give me the courage to talk about the hard subjects of drugs, sex, alcohol, and money with my child. Help me overcome any fear or embarrassment so that I can get the help I need. I need your wisdom. Thank you.

Notes

Notes

More from Tony and Nicole Davis

Visit *www.empowertoengage.com* to learn about Tony and Nicole, their ministry, and other available resources. This *Done Right* devotional book series includes:

Marriage Done Right Is Hard Work (But It's Worth It!)

This 31-day guide shows couples how to get the absolute best out of themselves and their marriage. As easy as it is today to walk away from the marriage covenant, it is actually just as easy to stay *if* we commit to living out marriage God's Way.

Leadership Done Right Is Hard Work (But It's Worth It!)

This 31-day guide challenges every person to lead *themselves* first and provides the strategies to do so. How we make decisions, conduct ourselves, and interact with others are the ultimate tests to our level of success in every area of life. Improving yourself, will make you the person that others willwant to follow.

To invite Tony and Nicole to speak at your next event, contact them with details:

Phone: 1-800-345-0805

Email: info@empowertoengage.com

Website: www.empowertoengage.com

Facebook: www.facebook.com/empowertoengage/

Printed in Great Britain
by Amazon